Assessment for learning: why, what and how?

Dylan Wiliam

First published in 2009 by the Institute of Education, University of London,
20 Bedford Way, London WC1H 0AL
www.ioe.ac.uk/publications

© Dylan Wiliam 2009

British Library Cataloguing in Publication Data:
A catalogue record for this publication is available from the British Library

ISBN 978 0 85473 788 8

Typeset by Keystroke, 28 High Street, Tettenhall, Wolverhampton

Printed by Elanders www.elanders.com

Institute of Education • University of London

Assessment for learning: why, what and how?

Dylan Wiliam

Professor of Educational Assessment

Based on an Inaugural Professorial Lecture delivered at the Institute of Education, University of London, on 24 April 2007

Professor Dylan Wiliam

Assessment for learning: why, what and how?

This professorial lecture takes the form of an argument. I want to convince you that raising achievement is important; that investing in teachers is the solution; that formative assessment should be the focus of that investment; and that teacher learning communities should be the mechanism. I will conclude the lecture with some thoughts on how we can put this into practice.

Raising achievement

The first step in the argument is to consider why we need to raise achievement. It is not because of Ofsted, league tables or what is sometimes called 'the standards agenda'. It is because raising achievement matters, both for individuals and for society. For the individual, higher achievement means an increased lifetime salary, improved health and longer life. For society it results in increased tax revenue, lower healthcare costs and reduced criminal justice costs.

For example, Hank Levin and colleagues at Teachers College, Columbia University recently showed that if we could help a single student who would otherwise have left school at 16 to stay on to the age of 18, the benefit to society would be $209,000. This breaks down as $139,000 in tax revenue, $40,500 in reduced healthcare costs from public assistance and $26,600 in reduced criminal justice costs (largely because they would be less likely to be imprisoned) and a variety of smaller contributions.

Raising student achievement also increases economic growth. Quantifying this inevitably requires some pretty heroic assumptions, but Eric Hanushek at the Hoover Institution has calculated that if we could raise student achievement by one standard deviation (equivalent to increasing their score by around 10 percentage points on a typical test) then within 30 years the extra growth in the economy would in effect mean that the whole of compulsory education would be free of charge. Raising achievement matters.

Given the importance of raising achievement – and this takes us on to the second part of the argument – it is hardly surprising that a great deal of political effort has been expended in the search for solutions. However, most of the efforts at reform to date have tended to focus on the aspects of educational systems that are easiest to change, rather than those that would make the most difference to young people. This appears to be largely driven by the fact that political timescales are much shorter than the timescales needed to effect educational reform. In America it is significant that a district superintendent – what we would call a Chief Education Officer – is in office for about 2.7 years on average and the tenure of the Secretary of State with responsibility for education in England is probably about the same. 'Making an impact' in education probably requires a focus on the things that are easy to change.

For example, in the United States, there appears to be a widespread belief that many high schools are too large, so that students get 'lost'. Accordingly, there has been a great deal of interest in the creation of smaller high schools – an initiative that has received a great deal of both political and financial support (particularly from the Bill and Melinda Gates Foundation). When I lived in Princeton, New Jersey, our state capital, Trenton, used some of this money to convert Trenton Central High School, with its 3,000 students, into six 500-student schools – in the same building. And they wondered why nothing changed.

Another solution that is popular in America is the creation of 'K-8' schools, by amalgamating middle schools with elementary schools. It is unclear why putting all those hormonal adolescents in with reception-age children is meant to be effective, but evaluations of such reforms indicate that they make little or no difference. In England also the emphasis appears to be on consolidation, with a great deal of interest in 'all-through' schools, catering for students from the ages of 3 to 19, and through the creation of federations of secondary schools led by 'Executive Headteachers'.

Many reforms are explicitly focused on diversifying the 'supply side' of education. In the United States this has commonly taken the form of 'Charter Schools' or the provision of educational 'vouchers' equivalent to the value of publicly funded education that parents can use to offset the cost of sending their children to private schools. In England, the focus has been on the creation of specialist schools, trusts, and academies. While many of these new kinds of educational provision have been successful in raising achievement, the improvements appear to be more to do with increased levels of resources (in the case of specialist schools) or changes in the nature of the students served by the school (in the case of academies).

Finally, there have been many initiatives involving computers – information technology has been about to revolutionise our classrooms for the last 30 years, and we're still waiting. As Larry Cuban noted, the history of computers in education is one of their being 'oversold and underused'. More recently, attention has focused on the interactive whiteboard, but as Ros Levačić and her colleagues here at the Institute of Education showed, the net impact of introducing interactive whiteboards into schools in London was zero. Moreover, in this particular study there was not just no evidence of impact, but rather *evidence of no impact.*

One reason that these ineffective solutions have been pursued for so long is because until recently, we have been looking in the wrong place for answers; it is only within the last few years that the data that allows us to ask the right kinds of questions have become available. Over the last 50 years or so there have been three distinct approaches to school effectiveness studies – what I call the three generations of school effectiveness research. The first generation focused exclusively on 'outputs' – students' scores on tests and examinations. In almost all countries outside Scandinavia, there is significant school-to-school variation in the achievement of students, leading to the conclusion that it is schools that make a difference. The key to increasing educational achievement is therefore to get more schools doing what the schools with the best scores are doing. However, as proponents of the second generation of school effectiveness research pointed out, taking into account differences in the intakes of different schools (using variables like free school meals or other proxies for social class) demographic factors account for over 90 per cent of the differences between schools' results. The message from the second generation of school effectiveness research is that schools do not make a difference, perhaps best encapsulated by Basil Bernstein's dictum that 'education cannot compensate for society'. However, as better data on the 'value added' by schools – the difference in achievement on entry to, and on exit from, the school – has become available, it is clear that while the differences between school, are indeed relatively small, classroom differences are quite large, even within the same school. The conclusion from this third and latest generation of school effectiveness research is that an effective school is little more than a school full of effective classrooms. It matters much less which school a child attends than which classrooms they are in at that school. There has been little dispute about this broad finding for quite a while, but it is only recently that it has become apparent how large that difference is.

In England, the variability at the classroom level appears to be as much as four times the variability at the school level. Children fortunate enough to be in the most effective classrooms will learn in six months what students in an average classroom learn in a year. And the children in the least effective classrooms will take two years to learn the same amount of material. In other words, there is a four-fold difference in the speed of learning between the most effective and least effective classrooms. The obvious factors – class size, the between-class grouping strategy, the within-class grouping strategy – make relatively little difference. What matters is the quality of the teacher.

Improving teacher quality

If we accept that teacher quality is the major determinant of how much progress students make, then we are left with a classic labour-supply issue, with two solutions. One is to replace existing teachers with better ones, as Ronald Reagan tried with air traffic controllers in the United States – sack them all and start again. The problem with this is that there is little evidence that better pay brings in better teachers nor that potentially better teachers are deterred by burdensome certification requirements (the majority of the studies find that the people brought in through these alternative routes perform no better, and often a good deal worse, than those coming through more traditional pathways). Even if we are able to raise the quality of new entrants into the profession through making teaching more attractive to graduates, the impact on average teacher quality is likely to be small, and will take many years to materialise.

The alternative to replacing existing teachers with better ones is to improve the effectiveness of those teaching already – what my former colleague at Educational Testing Service (ETS), Marnie Thompson, called 'the love the one you're with' strategy. This is the second step in the argument: that increasing educational achievement requires investment in teachers. There is evidence that this can be done but what we do not know is whether it can be done at scale, quickly, sustainably and at reasonable cost. This is what I and my colleagues have been working on for the last 20 years.

It is rare for the cost–benefits of different kinds of educational intervention to be considered in a disciplined way. For too long education research has been dominated by a paradigm where if the results of a study were statistically significant they would be published and it could be asserted that a particular intervention had a statistically significant impact. The problem with this 'cult of statistical significance' is that in a large experiment with hundreds of thousands of students, a change in the tenth decimal place can be statistically significant. Recently, more serious thought has been paid to the size of benefits, which has led to a degree of consensus, at least within the educational research community in the United States, that effect sizes, rather than statistical significance, should be reported. In the United Kingdom, however, the acceptance of this view has been slow, so that results are still reported because they are statistically significant rather than because they are substantive effects. Even when effect sizes are reported, this provides only half of the picture because they are of little relevance without some indication of the cost of securing the intervention at scale. What is important is the relative magnitudes of the costs and benefits.

Table 1 provides some examples of educational interventions, the likely impact on student learning, and their costs. Reducing class size does increase educational achievement but by less than most people assume, and at great cost. If class size is reduced by 30 per cent, for example by assigning three teachers rather than two across a group of 60 students so that the average class size is reduced from to 30 to 20, there will be four more months of learning per year (the smaller classes would achieve in 12 months what the larger classes would achieve in 16). This is an appreciable benefit, but it costs £20,000 per classroom (plus, across England, one would need to build 150,000 more classrooms). Even this amount of additional learning is not guaranteed because it is assumed that the additional 150,000 teachers who would be brought into the profession to enable class sizes to be reduced would be as effective as those already in post. A sobering illustration of the difficulty of implementing class-size reduction at scale is provided by the experience in California in the 1990s. The reduction in class size created a large number of new posts, many of which were in attractive and popular schools. A large number of experienced teachers applied for, and secured new posts in these schools, leaving many 'hard to staff' schools with even fewer teachers. To ensure that these schools were adequately staffed, many unqualified individuals were given 'emergency permits' so that in some districts, the effect of class-size reduction was actually to lower achievement.

Table 1 Cost/effect comparisons

Intervention	Extra months of learning per year	Cost per classroom per year
Class-size reduction (by 30%)	4	£20k
Increase teacher content knowledge from weak to strong	2	?
Formative assessment/assessment for learning	8	£2k

The important questions are therefore not 'Does class-size reduction work?', but 'By how much?', 'At what cost?', and 'What else might we do with the same money?'

One apparently obvious way to increase student achievement would be by increasing teacher content knowledge. This is a real concern in the United States where teacher content knowledge is often very weak, particularly in primary schools. But the impact of improvements in teacher content knowledge on student achievement is quite modest. For example, if we could improve a teacher's subject knowledge from well below average to well above average, or from average to outstanding (for the statistically minded, an increase of two standard deviations in teacher content knowledge), this would generate an extra two months' learning per year. Moreover, this is such an extraordinary increase in teacher content knowledge it is far from clear whether it is even achievable, let alone how much it would cost.

In comparison, getting teachers to make more use of formative assessment or assessment for learning (AfL) as it is sometimes called, has a much greater benefit. The research that Paul Black and I started reviewing in the 1990s, and the studies of implementation we conducted in Oxfordshire and Medway, suggest that a focus on formative assessment can generate as much as eight extra months of learning per year at a cost of only around £2,000 per classroom. This is around 20 times as cost-effective as class size reduction – if it can be achieved.

Formative assessment and assessment for learning (AfL)

The research in this area is relatively consistent. Gary Natriello and Terry Crooks both produced research reviews in the late 1980s. Natriello identified 91 references and Crooks identified 241. It is an indication of how difficult this area is to review that, although they were both researching within the same field, they only had nine references in common.

When Paul Black and I started conducting our own work in this area we discovered that there was no way to identify the relevant research without a manual search. We tried a number of automated searches, which returned either no references or 20,000. In the end we resorted to manual searches of every issue of 76 journals over a ten-year period. In our researches, we came across an important synthesis of work in the field undertaken by Kluger and DeNisi in 1996, which had reviewed over 3,000 studies on feedback in schools, colleges, and workplace settings; more recently, Jeffrey Nyquist reviewed 181 studies of feedback and formative assessment in higher education. Across all these reviews, the use of formative assessment is shown to have a consistent, substantial effect.

This is quite unusual, because in many areas of education research, when we ask 'Does it work?' the answer is often 'It depends – sometimes it does, sometimes it doesn't.' What is intriguing about the research on formative assessment is that whether the focus of study is Portugal or the United States, whether it is looking at 4-year-olds or 24-year-olds, whether it is looking at music or mathematics, there appear to be these consistent, substantial effects.

For an educational researcher, having governments adopt one's ideas as policy can be a mixed blessing. The idea of 'Records of Achievement', popular in the 1980s, was so diluted in its implementation that it was almost completely ineffective (and in some cases, probably counter productive). In a similar vein, Paul Black and I have wondered whether the same thing is happening to the idea of AfL, now firmly established as part of the government's National Strategy for education. While many authors use the terms 'assessment for learning' and 'formative assessment' interchangeably, Paul Black and I believe that there are important distinctions to be drawn. As we said in 2002:

> Assessment for learning is any assessment for which the first priority in its design and practice is to serve the purpose of promoting pupils' learning. It thus differs from assessment designed primarily to serve the purposes of accountability, or of ranking, or of certifying competence. An assessment activity can help learning if it provides information to be used as feedback, by teachers, and by their pupils, in assessing themselves and each other, to modify the teaching and learning activities in which they are engaged. Such assessment becomes 'formative assessment' when the evidence is actually used to adapt the teaching work to meet learning needs.

In other words, the term 'assessment for learning' speaks about the purpose of the assessment, while the term 'formative assessment' speaks about the function it actually serves. The focus on what the assessment actually does, rather than its intention, is implicit in the origins of the idea of feedback, developed over 60 years ago, in engineering.

Perhaps the canonical example of a feedback system is the room thermostat. In such a system there is a thermometer to measure the current temperature of the room, a device for setting the desired temperature of the room, and within the thermostat, a mechanism for comparing the actual temperature with the desired temperature. Finally, and most importantly, there is a cable that leads from the thermostat to the boiler. If the measured temperature is lower than the setting, it turns the boiler on. But central to this idea of a feedback loop is that *the device brings the system back into balance.* To an engineer, if the information fed back within the system does not have the capability of changing the system, it is not feedback. To an engineer, therefore, little of what is termed 'feedback' in schools would be recognised as such, because there is nothing in 'C – Must do better' to help the student improve. It is as if the cable from the thermostat to the boiler has been cut. The term 'feedback' has become so detached from its origins that it is routinely used to describe any report on current attainment. That is why the distinction between AfL and formative assessment is useful. What matters is how the information is used, not the purpose behind its collection.

Describing an assessment as formative is therefore a statement about the function that the feedback serves. Christine Harrison, a former colleague at King's College London, used to say that she saw plenty of formative intention in schools, but relatively little formative action. There are many people collecting information believing that it will be useful and that they will utilise it. But what they do with that information rarely meets the students' learning needs.

Perhaps predictably, because of the strong evidence showing that formative assessment is one of the most powerful ways of raising achievement, a number of test publishers in the United States have branded their traditional tests as 'formative assessments'. The idea is that students are tested every six to ten weeks in order to predict which students are likely to fail the state-wide test the following March. It doesn't tell teachers or administrators (or indeed students) what to do about it, but at least their impending failure comes with plenty of advance warning, so the administrators can begin to check that their CVs are up to date.

One response to this misuse of the term 'formative assessment' is to say that such tests aren't formative, and to lobby the test publishers to stop using the term, but given the profits at stake for the testing companies, I think this would be unlikely to succeed. Therefore, in order to be able to distinguish between effective and ineffective uses of formative assessment, it is helpful to distinguish between long-cycle, medium-cycle, and short-cycle formative assessments.

The possibility of good long-cycle formative assessments should not be discounted. If students' test scores are analysed and it is apparent that they are scoring poorly in one particular area of the curriculum, it makes sense to examine how that part of the curriculum is taught. While most people agree that 'teaching to the test' is not appropriate, making sure that students have been taught the material on which they are to be tested seems unexceptionable. However, if the curriculum is already well aligned to the national standards and the associated assessments, these kinds of intervention will have reasonably little effect.

Other useful assessments might have an even longer formative cycle-length. If a local authority adviser for primary schools found, by analysing the results of National Curriculum test results in mathematics, that students in her authority were performing much less well on items assessing shape and space, she might decide to make this topic a focus for teacher workshops in the coming year. Such an assessment could therefore be formative at the level of the system, rather than the individual student, and would not have an impact for at least a year.

Medium-cycle formative assessments focus on much shorter cycles of assessment, interpretation, and action – between one and four weeks. Done well, it results in greater student engagement in their own assessment and, when teachers meet together to talk about the outcomes, it can also bring improved teacher cognition about learning. But my own experience has been that getting teachers to talk about quality in students' work, while undoubtedly being a valuable professional development activity, rarely feeds through into changes in teachers' *classroom practice.* Teachers' thinking about what mathematics, science or English should be about ~~might be al~~tered radically, but too often, the result is just more topics (such as mathematical investigations or scientific explorations) added to the curriculum, rather than a change in how they teach – such approaches are treated as an addition to the load, rather than the vehicle.

However, unless the alignment of the curriculum to the national standards is very poor, unless the periodic assessments used by teachers are completely inappropriate, it is the shortest cycles of formative assessment – minute-to-minute and day-by-day – that have the greatest impact on student achievement. In other words, if students leave the classroom before teachers have used the information about their students' achievements to adjust their teaching, the teachers are already playing catch-up. If the teachers have not made adjustments by the time the students arrive the next day, it is probably too late. This 'short-cycle' formative assessment is powerful because it increases student engagement, and it improves the classroom practice of teachers, by making it more responsive to the students' needs.

While being clear about what kinds of timescales are involved in the most effective formative assessments is useful, in order to support teachers in developing these aspects of their practice, we need to go deeper and look at what, exactly, formative assessment is. There is now a developing consensus that it involves clarity over three processes: where learners are in their learning, where they are going, and the steps needed to get there. In addition, we need to keep in mind that within these processes there are different roles for teachers, learners, and their peers. Crossing the process dimension (where learners are in their learning, where they are going, how to get there) with that of the agent of the process (teacher, peer, learner) produces a grid of nine cells, which can be collapsed into the five 'key strategies' of formative assessment as shown in Figure 1.

Each of these five 'key strategies' provides a focal point for a range of related aspects of practice for teachers. In other words, they provide a starting point for a consideration of a number of wider issues in teaching, such as curriculum, psychology, and pedagogy.

The first, *clarifying, sharing and understanding* learning intentions provides the starting point because, before one can begin to design effective activities for

	Where the learner is going	Where the learner is right now	How to get there
Teacher	**1** Clarifying learning intentions and sharing and criteria for success	**2** Engineering effective classroom discussions, activities and tasks that elicit evidence of learning	**3** Providing feedback that moves learners forward
Peer	Understanding and sharing learning intentions and criteria for success	**4** Activating students as instructional resources for one another	
Learner	Understanding learning intentions and criteria for success	**5** Activating students as the owners of their own learning	

Figure 1 Aspects of formative assessment

learners, one has to be clear about what one wants the students to be able to do. One aspect of my work on formative assessment that has attracted criticism, both in the United Kingdom and the United States, is that I have completely eschewed any view of the curriculum within my definition of formative assessment. This is not because I do not think curriculum is not important, but rather it is because curriculum is not the best place to start when you want to change teacher practice. It is my experience that teachers feel that they have to teach the curriculum they have in front of them. If one tries to change that too quickly they are likely to say: 'Well, we have to teach what we are told to teach.' Even if one wanted to start teachers on the process of curriculum development, it is my experience that it is more productive to engage in that process via their pedagogy – the way they teach – rather than by challenging the curriculum head-on.

Engineering effective classroom discussions brings in classroom discourse and interactive whole-class teaching.

Feedback that moves learning forward emphasises that the major purpose of feedback is to provide the learner with guidance on what to do next, rather than telling her or him about what was deficient in the last piece of work – or as Douglas Reeves says, the difference between a medical and a post-mortem.

Activating students as learning resources for one another brings in collaborative and cooperative learning, reciprocal teaching (for example the work of Brown and Campione) and of course peer assessment.

Finally, *activating students as owners of their own learning* includes aspects of meta-cognition, motivation, interest, the way that learners attribute their successes and failures, and self-assessment.

The 'big idea' that ties all of this together is that evidence of student learning is used to adapt teaching and learning activities in order to meet student needs. This sounds straightforward, but it is far from common even in the best classrooms. In the United States, professional development materials that I developed with colleagues at the ETS are marketed under the title 'Keeping Learning on Track™'. The parallel with navigation highlights how strange some of our taken-for-granted classroom practices are. For example, I was flying back from the United States a few days ago and I was musing about what would happen if the pilot navigated the way that most teachers teach. We would set off from New York, with a bearing of around 070°, and with a planned flying time of 6.5 hours. After 6.5 hours the pilot would set the plane down at the nearest airport and ask the ground crew, 'Is this Gatwick?', and the ground crew might reply, 'No, it's Paris-Orly.' On hearing this the pilot would say to the passengers, 'I'm sorry, you've got to get off now because I have to get on to my next job.'

That is, after all, what happens in teaching. We teach a unit, and at the end of the teaching we give the students a test. If they score well on the test, then great, but if they have not, what do we say? 'Sorry. I know you didn't understand this, but we have to get on to Chapter 7 tomorrow. But don't worry, because we go over it again next year.' In each successive year of schooling, we go over the same material, with slightly more students picking it up each time – not so much a spiral curriculum as a circular one for many learners.

Here is an example of how profound the problem is. In the 1980s, as part of the Graded Assessment in Mathematics (GAIM) project directed by Margaret Brown, Alice Onion and I looked at the rate at which students' mathematical achievement increased as they got older. The work of the Concepts in Secondary Mathematics and Science (CSMS) project had shown that the proportion of students who could add simple fractions with unequal denominators (e.g. one-third and one-quarter) increased by only 8 per cent in two years. For more complex fractions, we found evidence from the Assessment of Performance Unit that approximately 27 per cent of students could add fractions reliably at the age of 11, and 35 per cent could do it by the age of 15. Therefore within four years the proportion of the population able to add fractions reliably increased by 8 per cent. This is equivalent to a 2 per cent increase in success rate each year. In other words, in a class of 25 students there is a 50 per cent chance that one child learns this in any one year. That is how slow the rate of improvement is under the current practice.

The three processes (where learners are in their learning, where they are going, how to get there), the three roles (teacher, peer, learner), and the five 'key strategies' they yield, form a kind of 'creation myth' for effective AfL. These five strategies, I would argue, collectively exhaust the terrain of AfL. If you are doing AfL, you are employing at least one of these five strategies, and if you're not employing at least one of these strategies, then you're probably not doing AfL.

The evidence that we have collected from small-scale investigations suggests that AfL provides a much more appropriate focus for investment in teacher professional development than anything else. This completes the third step in the argument. So how do we support teachers in developing these aspects of their practice?

Improving teacher practice

One of the great puzzles of educational research is why it has so little impact on the classroom practice of teachers; Aristotle's perspective on the nature of expertise (or intellectual virtue as he called it) is informative here. Aristotle identified three main intellectual virtues: *episteme*, *techne*, and *phronesis*. The first of these, *episteme* (science), is the knowledge of timeless universal truths. For example, the base angles of an isosceles triangle are always equal. Once you have proved this to be true, there is no need to check it tomorrow; it will still be true. The base angles of an isosceles triangle cannot be anything other than equal.

The second intellectual virtue, *techne* (craft), deals with the realm of things that are variable. For example, there is no one perfect form for a table, but the ability to make a table for a specific purpose is an important virtue. Yet it is the third intellectual value, *phronesis* (practical wisdom), that Aristotle regarded as the highest. As an example of *phronesis*, Aristotle gave the leadership of the state. For this task a person needs to be aware of important principles, but these must always be tempered by the knowledge of specific contexts.

This perspective is fruitful when we are thinking about the nature of expertise in teaching because governments, and agencies employed by governments, are often engaged in a search for 'what works'. However, in education 'what works' is not a particularly useful question to ask because almost everything works somewhere, and nothing works everywhere. The important question is, *'Under what conditions does a particular initiative work?'* Expertise in teaching would therefore appear to be mainly a matter of *phronesis* rather than *episteme* or, indeed, *techne*. This is why so much educational research appears to teachers either to tell them what they already know or something they know to be inappropriate to their particular circumstances.

If expertise in teaching is 'practical wisdom', how can we promote its development? The organisational theorists Ikujiro Nonaka and Hirotaka Takeuchi have looked at processes of knowledge creation and knowledge transfer in commercial organisations. In particular, they have explored the interplay of explicit and implicit or tacit knowledge (often described as the kind of knowledge that an organisation does not know it has until the people who have it leave).

Nonaka and Takeuchi outline four basic modes of knowledge conversion (see Figure 2). Perhaps the most familiar is the process they call 'combination' where one person communicates their explicit knowledge to another, for example, when one person tells another that lessons in a particular school are all of 40 minutes duration. A second form of knowledge conversion occurs when one person's implicit knowledge is picked up by others, implicitly, through a process of socialisation. An individual learns, 'That's the way things are done round here.'

'Externalisation' is a process in which one person's implicit knowledge is made explicit for the purpose of communication to another. When I started training teachers in the 1980s, I wasn't particularly helpful to the student teachers I was

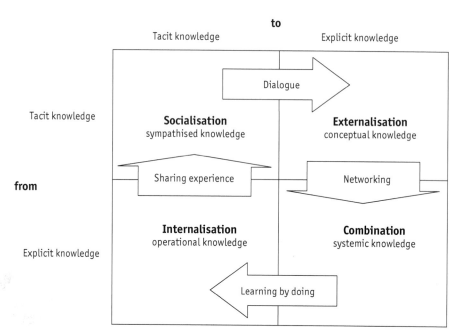

Figure 2 Knowledge 'transfer'
After Nonaka and Takeuchi (1995)

supporting because I had no way of describing what it was that I was doing. I had been reasonably successful as a practitioner, but had not developed a language for describing what I was doing. However, being forced to reflect on practice, and being forced to develop a language of description, I was developing a deeper understanding of my own practice.

Complementary to this is internalisation – the process of moving from explicit to implicit knowing. One example of this process is what happens when one is told how to do something, which creates a basic knowledge of the process, only for a much deeper understanding to emerge later – often months later. A friend of mine is a very keen golfer, and his coach was telling him that in order to improve his swing, he needed 'to quieten his lower body'. For weeks, he worked on trying to put this into practice, and eventually, he understood what his coach had meant, but only when he could actually do what his coach was suggesting. The phrase 'to quieten his lower body' looked like an instruction, but it was really a description of what it would feel like to have internalised this new knowledge, and make it into operational knowledge.

As well as these four modes of knowledge conversion, Nonaka and Takeuchi propose a 'knowledge spiral' that is generated by moving around the four modes of knowledge conversion through four processes: *sharing experience, dialogue, networking* and *learning by doing*. It is this model of knowledge creation and knowledge conversion that drives our approach to teacher professional development.

The fundamental insight contained in the Nonaka and Takeuchi model is that knowing something is not the same as being able to do it. In our conversations with teachers, Paul Black and I realised that many of the teachers knew the research we were talking about quite well. What they did not do was to enact this knowledge in their practice. The problem was not lack of knowledge but a lack of understanding of what it meant to do this in the classroom.

That is why I do not believe we should tell teachers what to do. This is not out of some misguided sense of wanting to be kind to teachers or to value their experience. If there were something that we could tell teachers to do with a guarantee that it would improve student outcomes, then there would be a strong case for telling them what to do (and perhaps even sacking those who refused!). After all, schools are there for students, not teachers. But telling teachers what to do doesn't work because it is impossible to prepare teachers for every situation they are going to face in the classroom. Telling teachers what to do does not work. Teaching is just too complex.

On the other hand, we also know that experience alone is not enough. Just leaving teachers to their own devices does not work either – if it were, then the most experienced teachers would generate the greatest progress in their students, and we know that is not true. Instead, what is needed are ways to support teachers to reflect on their practice in systematic ways, to build on their accessible knowledge base and, perhaps most importantly, to learn from mistakes.

Twenty years ago this would have resulted in a very gloomy prognosis, because there was relatively little evidence that it was possible to improve teacher practice. Huge amounts of money have been spent on professional development that has had relatively little impact on classroom practice. However, in recent years, it has become clear that the relative ineffectiveness of teacher professional development efforts in the past means nothing for what we might do in the future, because we have not engaged consistently in the kinds of activities that the research indicates are necessary in order to help teachers change their practice.

Content, *then* process

If we are to help teachers improve student outcomes, the starting point must be those things that make most difference to student outcomes. In other words, we start from the changes in teacher practice that make the most difference to students, and only then work out how to help teachers make the change – content, *then* process.

This is important because we can help teachers change a number of things about their practice. Some changes will benefit their students greatly, while others will not. For example, many teachers have become very interested in helping students understand their personal 'learning style' but there is little evidence that doing so has any impact on student achievement. If we are serious about improving educational achievement we have to help teachers focus on what matters, not just on what is interesting, expedient, or easy to change.

The professional development model that we have developed has two aspects related to content (i.e., what we want to help teachers change), and five related to process (how we help teachers change).

The first, and perhaps most important, element of our content model is evidence of efficacy. This is essential because without such evidence, teachers say, 'I would love to teach this way, but I can't because I've got to raise my test scores.' While test scores may not be the most important outcome of schooling, in the current climate it is essential that teachers know that if they increase their use of AfL, their students are likely to have higher achievement on tests and examinations. Fortunately, as discussed above, the evidence in favour of AfL is strong, and reasonably well organised.

The second content element of the model is a number of practical techniques for implementation in classrooms. Here are five examples.

For learning intentions, a very simple technique is to give students, before they are asked to write a story, examples of stories from last year's class – some good, some middling, and some weaker ones – and they then discuss, either in pairs, groups or as a whole class, what is good about the good ones.

To elicit evidence about current achievement for a whole class, mini 'dry-erase' boards, already in widespread use in many schools in Britain, can be used. For example a teacher who has just taught the students how to find equivalent fractions might ask the class to find a fraction between one-sixth and one-seventh. Many of the students will write down $\frac{1}{6\frac{1}{2}}$, which indicates some level of understanding of the concept, and provides a focus for subsequent whole-class discussion.

Techniques for feedback that moves learning forward typically involve ensuring that the feedback creates more work for the student. For example, a mathematics teacher once said to me, 'All this "comment only" marking that the research says is important is all very well in English lessons, but if you're marking a student's work and tick 15 of the answers as correct and mark five of them as incorrect then the child can work out for themselves that they've got 15 out of 20.' So I suggested that instead, the teacher could tell the student, 'Five of these are wrong. Find them and fix them.'

Many teachers have used the idea of 'traffic lights' to activate students as owners of their own learning. Typically, at the end of a piece of work, students are asked to indicate their confidence that they have achieved the learning objective for that piece of work with a traffic light, with green indicating confidence, yellow indicating partial understanding, and red signalling that the student is not at all confident they have learned what was intended. One teacher, who thought that getting such information at the end of the lesson was probably too late, gave each student three cups, coloured red, yellow, and green. At the beginning of the lesson the yellow and red cups are nested within the green cup. If a student thinks the teacher is going too fast, he or she can signal this to the teacher by showing the yellow cup. If a student wants to ask a question, then he or she shows the red cup. Why would any student show red? Because as soon as one student shows red, the teacher picks another student at random from all those showing either yellow or green cups, and that student has to come up to the front of the classroom to answer the question posed by the student who showed their red cup. In that way, it not only provides the teacher with information but also makes the students accountable and activates them as owners of their learning.

Finally, there are a number of ways in which teachers can increase the extent to which students act as learning resources for one another. For example, science teachers typically have a number of requirements for laboratory reports, including a margin for each page, headings being underlined, diagrams drawn in pencil and labelled and so on. One way to engage students in supporting each others' learning is to insist that before students are allowed to submit their report to the teacher they have to get a 'buddy' to certify that all the basic requirements have been satisfied by signing the 'pre-flight checklist'. The teacher then marks the assignment, and reports back to the student who wrote the report on the quality of the report, and to the 'buddy' on the extent to which they accurately assessed their partner's work in terms of how well the basic requirements had been met.

The second part of our professional development model focuses on the process – how we can support teachers in making greater use of AfL in their classrooms. From work with teachers over a ten-year period, five aspects of the process seem to be particularly important: choice, flexibility, small steps, accountability and support.

First, teachers need to be given a choice about what aspects of their practice to develop. It is often assumed that to improve, teachers should work on the weakest aspects of their practice, and for some teachers, these aspects may indeed be so weak that they should be the priority for professional development. But for most teachers, students will benefit more from teachers becoming even more expert in their strengths. In our work with teachers in Oxfordshire and Medway, one of the teachers, Derek (pseudonyms from the original study have been used in this section), was already quite skilled at conducting whole-class discussion sessions, but he was interested in improving this practice further. He is now one of the most skilled practitioners we have ever observed in this regard. A colleague of his at the same school, Philip, was much more interested in helping students develop skills of self-assessment and peer-assessment and he too is now highly skilled at these aspects of practice. To make Philip work on questioning, or to make Derek work on peer-assessment and self-assessment is unlikely to benefit their students as much as supporting each teacher to become excellent in their own way. Furthermore, when teachers themselves make the decision about what it is that they wish to prioritise for their own professional development, they are more likely to 'make it work'. In traditional 'top-down' models of teacher professional development, teachers are given ideas to try out in their own classrooms, but the response is too often, 'I tried what you told me and it didn't work.' However, if the choice about the aspects of practice to develop are made by the teacher, then the responsibility for ensuring effective implementation is shared by the teacher.

Second, teachers need the flexibility to be able to modify the AfL techniques they use to fit their own classroom context. The danger in this is that a teacher may so greatly modify an idea that it is no longer effective. In other words, the innovation suffers what Ed Haertel has called a 'lethal mutation'.

The third element of the process model is that of taking small steps. In implementing this professional development model, we have to accept that teacher learning is slow. This is, to borrow a rather well-known phrase, an 'inconvenient truth'. Social inequalities are everywhere, and the knowledge that high-quality education can largely alleviate many of these inequalities means that policy-makers are understandably in a hurry to make a difference. However, for changes in practice to be lasting, they must be integrated into a teacher's existing routines, and this takes time. Many of those involved in professional development are familiar with the experience of encouraging teachers to try out new ideas, and seeing them being enacted when they visit teachers' classrooms only to hear that as soon as they have left, the teachers revert to their former practices.

This reversion to well-rehearsed practices occurs because teaching is so complex that high-level performance relies on making a large proportion of the things that teachers do automatic. For learner drivers, changing gear and indicating right and steering all at the same time seem impossibly complicated, and if we try to undertake all these activities consciously, they are. Experienced drivers have practised these activities so many times that they function automatically. The up-side of this is that these automatic procedures take up little of the available cognitive processing power, leaving plenty for conducting a conversation with passengers. The down-side is that these automatic procedures are extremely hard to change.

Teaching is even more extreme than driving in this respect, because every teacher started out as a student. I often say to teachers that we learn most of what we know about teaching before our 18th birthdays. We learn the 'scripts' of school – the roles of teachers and students – by being in classrooms, and these patterns become 'hard-wired' into us. The research on parenting is similar. It shows that one can make a number of decisions about what kind of parent one wants to be. One can tell oneself that there are a number of things that one will never do as a parent. However, the number of such things we can hold in our minds at one time is limited, with the result that in emotionally fraught situations, one is relying on automatic responses – the ones that were laid down by 'being parented'.

This means that any kind of change in one's teaching practice is hard. But the kinds of changes I am calling for here are particularly hard, because they go 'against the grain' of current educational orthodoxy. In our pre-service courses with teachers, we talk about the importance of 'opening up' the classroom, providing space for students to talk, both because it is beneficial to their development, but also because by careful listening to what the students say, teachers can gain insights into their development. However, opening up the classroom in this way is seen by many teachers as 'giving up control' – faddish ideas being advocated by ivory tower academics who don't know what real teaching is. AfL practices would be hard to develop even in the most supportive climate, but are even harder when there is active hostility to their introduction. That is why, even if we are in a hurry to help teachers improve their practice, we should 'hasten slowly'.

The last two elements of the process model are support and accountability, which can be thought of as two sides of the same coin: supportive accountability. The idea here is that we create structures that, while making teachers accountable for developing their practice, also provide the support for them to do this. Developing one's practice of formative assessment is different from learning new facts. It requires developing new habits, and traditional models of teaching are much better at imparting knowledge than changing habits. As Ruth Sutton points out, if we want to change teachers' habits, we would do well to look at organisations such as *Weight Watchers*. After all, everyone who wants to lose weight knows they have to do two things: eat less and exercise more; the knowledge base for weight loss is actually very simple. What is hard is changing the habits that result in lack of time to exercise and to prepare food. In the same way if we are going to change what teachers do in classrooms then helping teachers change habits is as important as giving teachers new knowledge.

Clearly, creating this 'supportive accountability' could be done in a number of ways, but over the last six years or so, my colleagues and I have focused on one particular mechanism – teacher learning communities – as being particularly suited to the challenge of supporting teachers in their development of AfL.

Teacher learning communities

We have been exploring several different ways of constituting these teacher learning communities (TLCs), with a number of different patterns for meetings. While our early efforts worked well in the context for which they were designed, they needed radical revision to work in other contexts. However, after a number of false starts, and blind alleys, we believe we are now able to offer well-grounded advice about how to establish and support effective school-based TLCs to help teachers embed AfL in their practice.

Duration

The initial project should run for two years rather than one, because otherwise there is a danger that TLCs are seen as this year's innovation, with something else the priority for the following year and something different again the year after that.

Constitution

The teachers in the TLC need not be teaching the same subject (in secondary schools) or children of same age (in primary schools) but it does appear to be important for each member to have someone with substantially the same role in the group. While teachers often say that they value hearing from teachers of other subjects, or of children of other ages, it is hard for teachers to act as 'critical friends' if they know little about the subject or the age-range.

Size

Groups of between eight and 12 in size appear to be the most effective. When there are fewer than eight members of a TLC, occasional absences due to illness and other factors can reduce the size of the group to a point where there is insufficient diversity to generate effective discussion. If the group is much larger than 12, then constraints of time may mean that there is not time to hear back from each member of the group. In interviews, many participants have told us that it was the fact that they knew that they would be required to give to their colleagues an account of what they had been doing that made them prioritise working on changing their classroom practice over all the pressing concerns of a teacher's life.

Frequency

If meetings are too frequent, teachers will not have had sufficient time to try out new practices in their classrooms, and if the meetings are too infrequent, then the impetus for change begins to fade. Our experience is that one meeting a month is about right.

Format

One of the pervasive features of teacher professional development is a search for novelty. It seems to be accepted that teachers learn best from doing as many different kinds of things in their professional development as possible. This contrasts with many other professions, where, as Lee Shulman has pointed out, there are often *signature pedagogies* – agreed ways of organising learning that may not be perfect, but are good enough. The interesting thing about such signature pedagogies is that learners, be they students in law school or interns doing ward rounds, arrive knowing what to expect. As a result, the structure of the learning is taken for granted and falls into the background, while the learning itself is foregrounded. In contrast, much teacher education involves constant innovation, so that participants spend considerable amounts of time learning about the structures of learning. For this reason we suggest that every single monthly TLC meeting adopts the same format.

The format that we use currently, and which seems to be applicable in a wide range of contexts, involves six 'episodes' for each meeting.

Introduction (5 minutes)

Agendas for the meeting are circulated and the learning intentions for the meeting are presented.

Starter activity (5 minutes)

One of the things we have learned is that it can take teachers a while to 'tune in' to learning activities, especially at the end of a long teaching day. For this reason, we use a number of 'starter activities' that help people to focus. One way to do this is something we call the 'one minute whine' (something my partner Siobhan Leahy found particularly effective when working with teachers in dysfunctional local authorities). Using a stopwatch or an egg timer, each teacher is allotted one minute to 'sound off' about everything that is getting in the way of them doing their job – the students, the parents, the senior management of the school, and so on. Such 'venting' may seem negative, but without allowing the release of such emotions, there is a tendency for those issues to keep on resurfacing throughout the meeting. In order to prevent the meetings from consistently starting out on a negative note, some schools alternate the 'one minute whine' with opportunities for staff to say something positive they have seen recently.

Feedback (25 minutes)
Each teacher will have left the previous meeting with a commitment to the group to try something in their class. During the 'feedback' component of the meeting, each teacher gives a brief report on what they tried out and how it went. The rest of the group are required to listen appreciatively, and then to offer support to the individual in taking forward their own plans.

New learning about AfL (20 minutes)
In order to provide an element of novelty into each meeting of the TLC, and to provide a steady stream of new ideas, each meeting includes an activity that introduces some new ideas about AfL. This might be a task, a video to watch and discuss, or a 'book study' in which teachers will discuss a book chapter on AfL that they have read over the past month.

Personal action planning (15 minutes)
The penultimate activity of each session involves each of the participants planning in detail what they hope to accomplish before the next meeting. This may include trying out new ideas but it may simply be consolidation of techniques with which they have already experimented. This is also a good time for participants to plan any peer observations that they plan to undertake. It is our experience that if the participants leave the meeting without a definite date and time to observe one another, the peer observation is much less likely to take place.

Summary of learning (5 minutes)

In the last five minutes of the meeting, the group discusses whether they have achieved the learning intentions they set themselves. If they have not, there is time for the group to decide what to do about it.

One concern that many schools have about the organisation of these meetings is the degree of training that is required for the person who leads the group. In our experience, this is not a significant issue, because the group leader is not expected to be an expert in AfL. True, there is a need for someone to ensure the TLC meets regularly, to ensure all needed materials are ready for the meetings, to create and maintain a productive and non-judgemental tone during meetings and to ensure that the agenda is followed. However, it is our experience that meetings are much less successful when there is an AfL expert in the group, since they have a tendency to monopolise the conversation, and often tell others what to do. The idea of the TLC is that each participant comes to the meeting with their personal professional development plan, and gets the support of the group in achieving this.

Between meetings teachers are encouraged to participate in peer observations. In order to emphasise that these peer observations are primarily for the purpose of each individual teacher's professional development, and most emphatically not for assessing teacher performance, we suggest that it is the person who is being observed that specifies what is being looked for and also what evidence should be collected. This minimises the likelihood that the person conducting the observation introduces their own agenda in the observation and says: 'This is what you *ought* to be doing. . .' The distinction between these kinds of peer observations and traditional 'performance management' can be further reinforced by making it clear that any notes made during the lesson by the observer are the property of the teacher being observed.

The crucial point in all this is that TLCs are regarded as a means to an end rather than an end in themselves. If the research outlined earlier had shown that the most important lever for change was increasing teachers' content knowledge, then TLCs would be a rather weak mechanism. Some form of direct teaching of the content knowledge would be likely to be far more effective.

However, because the research shows that in fact, it is teachers' classroom practices that have the most impact on learners, we have to develop the models of professional development best suited to changing teachers' habits.

This professional development model is slightly different from the normal 'research and disseminate' model that is generally espoused for education. In the traditional model, researchers generate cognitive or affective insights into learning, and then try to communicate these insights to teachers. In the model that Paul Black and I have developed, our design process begins with our cognitive and affective insights into learning, and we have then built these into a theory of formative assessment (as in Figure 1 above). We then manifested the theory in terms of a set of components that teachers could adopt and implement (the classroom techniques discussed earlier). In turn, teachers then adopt these components, which they then integrate into their practice, which then results in cognitive and affective insights for the teacher. This is shown diagrammatically in Figure 3 below.

This resonates with the views of Millard Fuller, the founder of *Habitat for Humanity*, who suggested that, at least in matters of environmental sustainability, it is generally easier to get people to *act* their way into a new way of

Our design process

Teachers' implementation process

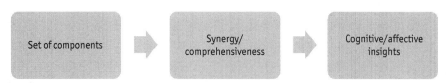

Figure 3 Design and intervention

thinking than it is to get people to *think* their way into a new way of *acting*. It seems to me that most teacher professional development – and indeed much of my own efforts over the last 20 years – has been focused on getting teachers to think their way into a new way of acting. For some aspects of practice this may have been appropriate, but for something as intrinsic to teachers' day-to-day and minute-to-minute classroom practice as AfL, it is more appropriate to support teachers in acting their way into a new way of thinking.

Taking it to scale

The argument so far has shown that AfL is likely to be the most cost-effective way to improve student outcomes, but that it is likely to require very different models of teacher professional development from those currently in use. The evidence from small-scale trials is that the effects that the literature shows are possible are indeed achievable even when AfL is used in real classrooms as opposed to laboratory settings, even when the intervention takes place over a school year rather than the much shorter timescales that are used in many studies, and even when the outcomes are measured with large-scale mandated assessments, rather than teacher-produced measures. What is much less clear is how to achieve these effects at scale – across 300,000 classrooms in England, or across 2 million classrooms in the United States.

Indeed, the issue of implementing educational improvements at scale seems to attract the interest of relatively few researchers. At national conferences such as those of the American Educational Research Association (AERA) and the British Educational Research Association (BERA) it is common to find teachers talking about research undertaken with a small group of teachers over extended periods of time, charting their development, and exploring ways of understanding outstanding practice. To over-simplify somewhat, while we don't know everything about excellent teaching, we know quite a lot about what makes good teaching; what we know far less about is how to get more of it.

In designing ways of supporting teachers to develop their practice of formative assessment across an educational system, the first principle Marnie Thompson and I adopted was that of 'in-principle scalability' – the design of the intervention had to be designed so that it could, in principle, be scaled to at least 10,000 classrooms. The intervention need not be scalable at the outset, but any aspect of the intervention that could, under any set of reasonable assumptions, not be implemented at scale was ruled out.

The second principle was a commitment to a single model for the whole school. I am constantly surprised by the 'Balkanised' nature of many schools' approaches to professional development, especially in secondary schools. The mathematics teachers are doing one thing, the science teachers doing another, and the history teachers something else entirely. It is difficult and confusing for the students, and you do not get any of the synergies that can arise from common approaches to teaching and talking about teaching. However, while we were committed to a single model for the whole school, we had also to honour the specificities of age and subject. Teaching 5-year-olds is not the same as teaching 10-year-olds, and teaching mathematics is not the same as teaching history.

Our other principles were based on the work of Cynthia Coburn, who emphasised that scalability has four important dimensions: the depth of the reforms, the sustainability, the spread, and the shift in reform ownership (away from the designers of the reform and towards those who implement it).

The other requirement we felt was necessary for an intervention to be scalable was a way of ensuring that it could be implemented successfully in different schools and different local education authorities, each of which has their own particular circumstances. To do this we realised that we needed to be able to articulate precisely how we believed our intervention would work, so that any preconditions that would be essential for success could be specified, and any features of the local context that would prevent effective implementation could be removed or mitigated.

To do this, we drew on the work of colleagues at ETS, led by Siobhan Leahy, who had been developing the idea of 'logic models' for educational interventions. The development of educational interventions takes a long time, and conducting randomised trials of their efficacy is expensive and time-consuming, so some way of evaluating the likely efficacy of an intervention, before incurring the expense of proofs of concept and randomised controlled trials, is necessary.

The formulation that Siobhan Leahy and her colleagues used for presenting a logic model involves both a theory of action and an evidence base. The logic model for the 'Keeping Learning on Track™' professional development package is shown in Figure 4. On the left are the components of the intervention, and on the right is a single box: improved student learning. In between the 'theory of action' of the intervention is specified in terms of teacher outcomes and student outcomes. For example, providing teachers with training on how to give feedback is intended to improve the feedback that teachers provide for their students. In turn, the theory of action specifies that students will use this feedback to improve their assignments, and the intended outcome is improved student learning. It is important to note that the theory of action is not necessarily a description of how the intervention works. It is a protocol for articulating beliefs about how the intervention will have worked, if it works.

The second element of the logic model is the evidence base. Once the 'theory of action' of the intervention has been articulated, we can begin to assemble the evidence that it is, indeed, likely to work in the way proposed, by reference to the research literature. Each arrow in Figure 4 is numbered, and these numbers refer to research studies – ideally from random-allocation trials – that show that the particular step in the model is plausible (e.g., that if teachers do provide students with better feedback, students will improve their assignments).

By specifying how the intervention works, the logic model allows us to be clear about what absolutely needs to be in place (and also, possibly, what must not be present!) for the intervention to work. Things that are not in the logic model are therefore deemed to be less important. We call this approach 'tight, but loose'.

In many educational interventions – such as the 'Effective Schools' movement in the United States – the absolute requirements (the 'tight' part) were quite minimal, which made the movement attractive, but of limited impact. In contrast, the Montessori method, which is undoubtedly effective, specifies in great detail how the approach is to be implemented (so the 'tight' part is relatively large) which is daunting for many schools. Our 'tight, but loose' formulation combines an obsessive adherence to central design principles as articulated in the logic model (the tight part) with accommodations to the needs, resources,

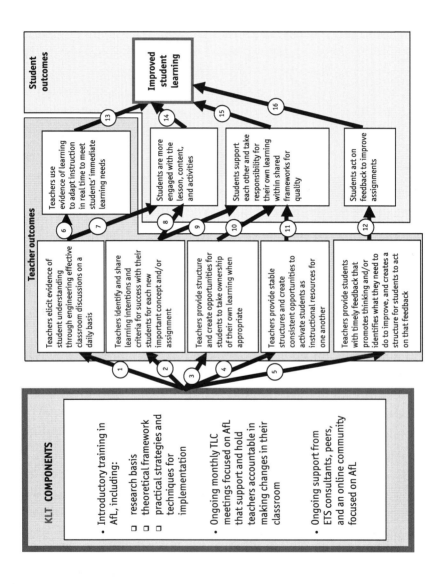

Figure 4 Logic model for 'Keeping Learning on Track™' (KLT)

Source: Leahy, Leusner and Lyon (2005)

constraints and particularities that occur in any school (the loose part), but only where the latter does not conflict with a theory of action.

For example, in our approach to supporting teachers in developing AfL, we are 'tight' about giving teachers choice. In one school the headteacher said that he would like everyone to work on questioning for the first year, which was a clear contradiction of our approach to TLCs. However, we were not at all concerned about where the meetings are held, or whether they were held during school time or at the end of the day. Similarly, we are 'tight' about the five key strategies outlined in Figure 1 – if teachers are not focusing on one of the strategies outlined above, then they are taking a risk that they are straying beyond what the research base suggests will improve student outcomes. On the other hand, we are 'loose' about the techniques – these are entirely a matter for the teachers to choose. We are tight about the 'Feedback' section in each meeting of the TLC and about the action planning, but loose about the 'New learning' section. We are 'tight' about the size of the TLC because each of the teachers must have the opportunity (indeed, are required) to speak, but we are 'loose' about its composition.

We have had a number of small-scale implementations in the United States. In Ohio, we worked with the ten lowest performing schools in Cleveland Municipal School District (out of a total of 76 schools). In the other 66 schools, approximately half improved their results year on year. In the ten schools we were working with every one of them improved their results. Now there is, of course, a likelihood that some of this is attributable to the effect of regression to the mean, but even controlling for this, the effect appears to be similar to what we found in our earlier work in Oxfordshire and Medway. Other pilots are taking place in Vermont, California, North Carolina and Texas, and the results are promising. We have also begun to explore local-authority based approaches to scaling up AfL in Scotland, working with the Tapestry Partnership, and in England with the Specialist Schools and Academies Trust (SSAT).

Conclusion and future direction

As I said at the beginning of this lecture, my aim was to assemble an argument. I have, I hope, shown how important it is that we improve educational outcomes for young people, and that the only plausible way to do this, at least in the short to medium term, is to invest in our existing teachers, through sustained professional development. To be effective, teacher professional development must address both what teachers do in the classroom and how it is that teachers can change. We think that formative assessment or AfL supported with TLCs provides a uniquely powerful point of leverage for improving teacher practice, and one that can be implemented widely. I believe that we are on the verge of having an effective, and scalable model for teacher professional development.

As a result, I am now more optimistic than I have ever been before in my career as a professional developer that we can make a difference to schools at scale. This is not the only important factor, but the focus on AfL does provide a kind of 'Trojan horse' into wider issues of pedagogy, psychology, and curriculum.

That is why I think that if you are serious about raising student achievement then you have to be focusing on AfL, and if you are not focusing on AfL you are probably not serious about raising student achievement.

Notes

Page 1

'For example, Hank Levin and colleagues at Teachers College, Columbia University recently showed. . .': Levin, H.M., Belfield, C., Muennig, P., and Rouse, C. (2007) *The Costs and Benefits of an Excellent Education for all of America's Children.* New York: Teachers College Press.

Page 2

'Quantifying this inevitably requires some pretty heroic assumptions, but Eric Hanushek at the Hoover Institution has calculated. . .': Hanushek, E.A. (2004) *Some Simple Analytics of School Quality* (Vol. W10229). Washington, DC: National Bureau of Economic Research.

'"Making an impact" in education probably requires a focus on the things that are easy to change': Snider, J.H. (2006) 'The superintendent as scapegoat'. *Education Week*, 25(18), 40, 31, 11 January.

Page 3

'While many of these new kinds of educational provision have been successful in raising achievement, the improvements appear to be more to do with increased levels of resources (in the case of specialist schools). . .': Mangan, J., Pugh, G., and Gray, J. (2007) 'Examination performance and school expenditure in English secondary schools in a dynamic setting'. Paper presented at the Annual Conference of the British Educational Research Association, London, UK.

'As Larry Cuban noted, the history of computers in education is one of their being "oversold and underused"': Cuban, L. (2001) *Oversold and Underused: Computers in the classroom*. Harvard: Harvard University Press.

'More recently, attention has focused on the interactive whiteboard, but as Ros Levačić and her colleagues here at the Institute of Education showed. . .': Moss, G., Jewitt, C., Levačić, R., Armstrong, V., Cardini, A., and Castle, F. (2007) *The Interactive Whiteboards, Pedagogy and Pupil Performance Evaluation: An Evaluation of the Schools Whiteboard Expansion (SWE) Project: London Challenge*. Annealed: DfES Publications.

'In almost all countries outside Scandinavia, there is significant school-to-school variation in the achievement of students': McGaw, B. (2008) 'The role of the OECD in international comparative studies of achievement'. *Assessment in Education: Principles Policy and Practice*, 15(3), 223–43.

Page 4

'The message from the second generation of school effectiveness research is that schools do not make a difference, perhaps best encapsulated by Basil Bernstein's dictum that "education cannot compensate for society"': Bernstein, B. (1970) 'Education cannot compensate for society'. *New Society*, 15(387), 344–7, 26 February.

'In England, the variability at the classroom appears to be as much as four times the variability at the school level': Slater, H., Davies, N. and Burgess, S. (2008) *Do Teachers Matter? Measuring the variation in teacher effectiveness in England* (CMPO Working Paper 09/212). Bristol: University of Bristol Institute of Public Affairs.

'Children fortunate enough to be in the most effective classrooms': Hanushek, E.A. (2004) 'Some simple analytics of school quality (Vol. W10229). Washington, DC: National Bureau of Economic Research.

Page 5

'The alternative to replacing existing teachers with better ones is to improve the effectiveness of those teaching already – what my former colleague at Educational Testing Service (ETS), Marnie Thompson, called "the love the one you're with" strategy': Wiliam, D. and Thompson, M. (2007) 'Integrating assessment with instruction: what will it take to make it work?' In C. A. Dwyer (ed.), *The Future of Assessment: Shaping teaching and learning*. Mahwah, NJ: Lawrence Erlbaum Associates, 53–82.

'The problem with this "cult of statistical significance" . . .': Ziliak, S. and McCloskey, D. (2008) *The Cult of Statistical Significance*. Ann Arbor, MI: University of Michigan Press.

Page 6

'To ensure that these schools were adequately staffed, many unqualified individuals were given "emergency permits" so that in some districts, the effect of class-size reduction was actually to lower achievement': Jepsen, C. and Rivkin, S. (2002) 'What is the tradeoff between smaller classes and teacher quality?' NBER Working Paper series. Cambridge, MA: National Bureau of Economic Research.

Page 7

'For example, if we could improve a teacher's subject knowledge from well below average to well above average, or from average to outstanding (for the statistically minded, an increase of two standard deviations in teacher content knowledge), this would generate an extra two months' learning per year': Hill, H.C., Rowan, B. and Ball, D.L. (2005) 'Effects of teachers' mathematical knowledge for teaching on student achievement'. *American Educational Research Journal*, 42(2), 371–406.

'The research in this area is relatively consistent. Gary Natriello and Terry Crooks both produced research reviews in the late 1980s': Natriello, G. (1987) 'The impact of evaluation processes on students'. *Educational Psychologist*, 22(2), 155–75; Crooks, T. J. (1988) 'The impact of classroom evaluation practices on students'. *Review of Educational Research*, 58(4), 438–81.

'When Paul Black and I started conducting our own work in this area we discovered that there was no way to identify the relevant research without a manual search.' For further discussion see: Black, P.J. and Wiliam, D. (1998) 'Inside the black box: raising standards through classroom assessment'. *Phi Delta Kappa*, 80(2), 139–48; Wiliam, D., Lee, C., Harrison, C., and Black, P.J. (2004) 'Teachers developing assessment for learning: impact on student achievement'. *Assessment in Education: Principles, Policy, and Practice*, 11(1), 49–65.

Page 8

'In our researches, we came across an important synthesis of work in the field undertaken by Kluger and DeNisi in 1996, which had reviewed over 3,000 studies on feedback in schools, colleges, and workplace settings, and more recently, Jeffrey Nyquist reviewed 181 studies of feedback and formative assessment in higher education.' See: Kluger, A.N. and DeNisi, A. (1996) 'The effects of feedback interventions on performance: a historical review, a meta-analysis, and a preliminary feedback intervention theory'. *Psychological Bulletin*, 119(2), 254–84; Nyquist, J.B. (2003) 'The benefits of reconstruing feedback as a larger system of formative assessment: a meta-analysis'. Unpublished MSc thesis, Vanderbilt University, Nashville, TN.

'Assessment for learning is any assessment for which the first priority in its design and practice is to serve the purpose of promoting pupils' learning': Wiliam, D., Black, P.J., Harrison, C., Lee, C., and Marshall, B. (2002) *Working inside the Black Box: Assessment for learning in the classroom 2002*. London: King's College London, Department of Education and Professional Studies.

Page 11

'Crossing the process dimension (where learners are in their learning, where they are going, how to get there) with that of the agent of the process (teacher, peer, learner) produces a grid of nine cells, which can be collapsed into the five "key strategies" of formative assessment. . .': see also Wiliam, D. and Thompson, M. (2007) 'Integrating assessment with instruction: what will it take to make it work?' In C. A. Dwyer (ed.), *The Future of Assessment: Shaping teaching and learning*. Mahwah, NJ: Lawrence Erlbaum Associates, 53–82.

Page 13

'*Activating students as learning resources for one another* brings in collaborative and cooperative learning, reciprocal teaching (for example the work of Brown and Campione). . .': Brown, A.L. and Campione, J.C. (1992) 'Students as researchers and teachers'. In J.W. Keefe and H.J. Walberg (eds), *Teaching for Thinking*. Reston, VA: National Association of Secondary School Principals, 49–57.

'In the United States, professional development materials that I developed with colleagues at the Educational Testing Service are marketed under the title "Keeping Learning on Track™"'. See Wiliam, D. (2007) 'Keeping learning on track: formative assessment and the regulation of learning'. In F.K. Lester, Jr (ed.), *Second Handbook of Mathematics Teaching and Learning*. Greenwich, CT: Information Age Publishing, 1053–98.

'The work of the Concepts in Secondary Mathematics and Science (CSMS) project had shown that the proportion of students who could add simple fractions with unequal denominators (e.g. one-third and one-quarter) increased by only 8 per cent in two years.': Hart, K.M. (1981) 'Fractions'. In K.M. Hart (ed.), *Children's Understanding of Mathematics: 11–16* (66–81). London: John Murray, 79.

Page 14

'One of the great puzzles of educational research is why it has so little impact on the classroom practice of teachers. . .': Lagemann, E.C. (2000) *An Elusive Science: The troubling history of education research*. Chicago, IL: Chicago University Press.

'Aristotle identified three main intellectual virtues: *episteme*, *techne*, and *phronesis*': Aristotle (2000) *The Nicomachean Ethics* (R. Crisp, Trans.). Cambridge, UK: Cambridge University Press. See also Wiliam, D. (2008) 'Comments on Bulterman-Bos: What should education research do, and how should it do it?'. *Educational Researcher*, 37, 432–8.

Page 15

'The organisational theorists Ikujiro Nonaka and Hirotaka Takeuchi have looked at processes of knowledge creation and knowledge transfer in commercial organisations . . .': Nonaka, I. and Takeuchi, H. (1995) *The Knowledge-Creating Company: How Japanese companies create the dynamics of innovation*. New York: Oxford University Press.

Page 21

'In our work with teachers in Oxfordshire and Medway. . .': Black, P., Harrison, C., Lee, C., Marshall, B., and Wiliam, D. (2003) *Assessment for Learning: Putting it into practice.* Buckingham: Open University Press.

'In other words, the innovation suffers what Ed Haertel has called a "lethal mutation"'. This is a personal communication quoted in: Brown, A.L. and Campione, J.C. (1996) 'Psychological theory and the design of innovative learning environments: on procedures, principles, and systems'. In L. Schauble and R. Glaser (eds), *Innovations In Learning: New Environments for Education.* Hillsdale, NJ: Lawrence Erlbaum Associates, 291–2. Haertel outlines this in the following way:

> Research-based programs of the latter part of the century have emphasised the central role of process. In FCL [Fostering Communities of Learners] for example, students are required to practice research-like activities, to become involved in systems of activity that lead them to engage in understanding texts, writing to communicate, engaging in domain-situated problem-solving, and so forth. To put these processes into practice, theorists and practitioners often devise specific procedures aimed to introduce and support them. These procedures are based on and embody specific learning principles. It is the embodiment and enactment of these principles, rather than the surface procedures, that is important. But this in turn requires that those using the procedures understand the underlying principles, else the procedures can degenerate into a modified activity unrelated to the guiding principles. Some modifications so depart from the original philosophy that they can be termed 'lethal mutations' (E.H. Haertel, personal communication, 1994).

Page 23

'As Ruth Sutton points out, if we want to change teachers' habits, we would do well to look at organisations such as *Weight Watchers*.' Personal communication.

Page 25

'This contrasts with many other professions, where, as Lee Shulman has pointed out, there are often *signature pedagogies* – agreed ways of organising learning that may not be perfect, but are good enough': Shulman, L.S. (2005) 'Signature pedagogies in the professions' *Daedalus,* 134(3), 52–9.

Page 29

'The evidence from small-scale trials is that the effects that the literature shows. . .': Wiliam, D., Lee, C., Harrison, C., and Black, P. (2004) 'Teachers developing assessment for learning: impact on student achievement'. *Assessment in Education: Principles, Policy, and Practice*, 11(1), 49–65; Hayes, V.P. (2003) 'Using pupil self-evaluation within the formative assessment paradigm as a pedagogical tool'. Unpublished doctoral dissertation, University of London; Clymer, J.B. and Wiliam, D. (2006/2007) 'Improving the way we grade science'. *Educational Leadership*, 64(4), 36–42.

Page 30

'Our other principles were based on the work of Cynthia Coburn, who emphasised that scalability has four important dimensions. . .': Coburn, C. (2003) 'Rethinking scale: moving beyond numbers to deep and lasting change'. *Educational Researcher*, 32(6), 3–12.

'To do this, we drew on the work of colleagues at ETS, led by Siobhan Leahy, who had been developing the idea of "logic models" for educational interventions': Leahy, S., Lyon, C., Thompson, M., and Wiliam, D. (2005) 'Classroom assessment: minute-by-minute and day-by-day'. *Educational Leadership*, 63(3), 8–24.

Page 31

'We call this approach "tight, but loose"': Thompson, M. and Wiliam, D. (2008) 'Tight but loose: a conceptual framework for scaling up school reforms'. In E.C. Wylie (ed.), *Tight but Loose: Scaling up teacher professional development in diverse contexts* (Vol. RR-08-29, pp. 1–44). Princeton, NJ: Educational Testing Service.

'In contrast, the Montessori method, which is undoubtedly effective. . .': Lillard, A. and Else-Quest, N. (2006) 'Evaluating Montessori education'. *Science*, 313(5795), 1893–4.

Page 32

Figure 4 is taken from Leahy, S., Leusner, D.M. and Lyon, C.J. (2005) *Providing a Research Basis for ETS Products*. Princeton, NJ: Educational Testing Service.